W9-AOS-004

Great National Soccer Teams / Grandes selecciones del fútbol mundial

GERMANY / ALEMANIA

José María Obregón

English translation: Megan Benson

PowerKiDS press.

Editorial Buenas Letras™
New York

Published in 2010 by The Rosen Publishing Group, Inc.
29 East 21st Street, New York, NY 10010

First Edition

Editor: Nicole Pristash
Book Design: Julio Gil
Photo Researcher: Jessica Gerweck

Photo Credits: Cover Christof Koepsel/Bongarts/Getty Images; back cover, pp. 5, 9 Bob Thomas/ Getty Images; pp. 7, 11 Rolls Press/Popperfoto/Getty Images; pp. 13, 21 (right) Popperfoto/Getty Images; pp. 15, 21 (left) Bongarts/Getty Images; p. 17 Mark Sandten/Bongarts/Getty Images; p. 19 Daniel Garcia/AFP/Getty Images; p. 21 (flag) Shutterstock.com; p. 21 (middle) Allsport UK/ Allsport/Getty Images.

Library of Congress Cataloging-in-Publication Data

Obregón, José María, 1963–
   Germany = Alemania / José María Obregón. — 1st ed.
      p. cm. — (Great national soccer teams = Grandes selecciones nacionales de fútbol)
   Includes index.
   ISBN 978-1-4042-8087-8 (library binding) — ISBN 978-1-4358-2493-5 (pbk.) —
ISBN 978-1-4358-2494-2 (6-pack)
   1. Soccer—Germany—Juvenile literature. 2. Soccer teams—Germany—Juvenile literature. I. Title.
II. Title: Alemania.
   GV944.G3O37 2010
   796.3340943—dc22
                                        2008053958

Manufactured in the United States of America

CONTENTS

CONTENIDO

The German national soccer team has proved to be one of the most successful soccer teams in the world. Germany has won the **World Cup** three times. The team has also finished in the top three in 10 World Cups!

La selección de fútbol de Alemania ha demostrado ser uno de los equipos de fútbol más exitosos del mundo. Alemania ha ganado en tres ocasiones la **Copa del Mundo**. ¡Además, Alemania ha terminado en los tres primeros lugares en 10 Copas del Mundo!

German goalkeeper Sepp Maier is shown here celebrating after winning the World Cup in 1974.

Aquí vemos al portero, Sepp Maier, levantar la copa después de ganar la Copa del Mundo 1974.

Throughout its history, Germany's national soccer team has had its share of talented players. German players Lothar Matthäus, Gerd Müller, Jürgen Klinsmann, Oliver Kahn, and Franz Beckenbauer are among the best players in soccer history.

A lo largo de la historia, la selección alemana ha contado con grandes jugadores. Jugadores alemanes como Lothar Matthäus, Gerd Müller, Jürgen Klinsmann, Oliver Kahn y Franz Beckenbauer se encuentran entre los mejores jugadores en la historia del fútbol.

With 68 goals, Gerd Müller (right) is Germany's all-time top scorer.

Gerd Müller (derecha) es el mejor anotador alemán de la historia con 68 goles.

The German team's success is due to the strength and speed of its players. The team never gives up! German fans are proud of their team and its **determination**. In Germany, the team is known as the *nationalelf*, or national 11.

El éxito de la selección alemana se debe a la gran fuerza y velocidad de sus jugadores. ¡La selección alemana nunca se rinde! Los aficionados alemanes están orgullosos de la **determinación** de su equipo. En Alemania, la selección se conoce como el Nationalelf, o la oncena nacional.

Here Jürgen Klinsmann (left) is shown jumping for the ball.

Aquí, Jürgen Klinsmann (izquierda) salta por el balón con gran fuerza.

Germany won its first World Cup in 1954. Germans, though, will never forget the team's loss in an **exciting** match called the Game of the Century. Germany played against Italy in the 1970 World Cup semifinal. Germany lost, 4–3, in overtime, or extra time added to the end of the game.

Alemania ganó su primera Copa del Mundo en 1954, pero los alemanes nunca olvidarán su famosa derrota en el llamado Juego del Siglo. Alemania jugó contra Italia la semifinal de la Copa del Mundo de 1970. El partido se decidió en tiempos extras y Alemania perdió por 4 goles a 3.

Italian player Tarcisio Burgnich (right, in dark shirt) scores a goal during the Game of the Century.

El jugador italiano, Tarcisio Burgnich (derecha, en camiseta oscura) anota un gol durante el Juego del Siglo.

11

One of Germany's great players is Franz Beckenbauer. During the Game of the Century, he played with a **dislocated** shoulder. During 12 years with the German team, Beckenbauer played in three World Cups, with one win in 1974. He also played on the team that won the 1972 European Football Championship.

Ningún otro jugador representa el fútbol alemán mejor que Franz Beckenbauer. En el Juego del Siglo, Beckenbauer jugó a pesar de tener un hombro **dislocado**. Durante 12 años con la selección nacional, Beckenbauer jugó tres Copas del Mundo, ganando en 1974. Además, Beckenbauer ganó la Eurocopa 1972.

Franz Beckenbauer, shown here, raises his arms in celebration after winning the 1974 World Cup.

Aquí vemos a Franz Beckenbauer levantando los brazos tras ganar la Copa del Mundo de 1974.

13

Beckenbauer also became the national team's coach. In 1990, Beckenbauer helped Germany win their third World Cup, in Italy. With this win, Beckenbauer became the second man in history to win a World Cup as a player and as a coach.

Beckenbauer también fue entrenador de la selección de Alemania. Beckenbauer llevó a Alemania a ganar su tercera Copa del Mundo en Italia 1990. Así, Beckenbauer se convirtió en la segunda persona en la historia en ganar la copa como jugador y entrenador.

Franz Beckenbauer (left) and the German team arrive in Germany after winning their third World Cup.

Franz Beckenbauer (izquierda) y el equipo alemán llegan a casa tras ganar su tercera Copa del Mundo.

In 1996, Germany became the first country to win the European Football Championship three times. Germany beat the Czech Republic in the final game. Germany was losing the game, 1–0, but player Oliver Bierhoff came into the game and scored two goals, winning the title for the *nationalelf*.

En 1996, Alemania se convirtió en el primer país en ganar la Eurocopa en tres ocasiones. Alemania jugó la final contra la República Checa y el héroe del partido fue Oliver Bierhoff. Alemania perdía el partido 1 por 0, cuando Bierhoff entró como sustituto para anotar dos goles y darle la copa al Nationalelf.

Oliver Bierhoff´s two goals won the title for Germany at the 1996 European Football Championship.

Dos goles de Oliver Bierhoff le dieron el triunfo a Alemania en la Eurocopa de 1996.

17

When the World Cup was held in Germany in 2006, the country dreamed of winning their fourth title at home. After a good start, Germany played Italy in the semifinals. As had happened 26 years before, in the Game of the Century, Germany lost the game in overtime.

Alemania organizó la Copa del Mundo en 2006 y el país soñaba con ganar su cuarta Copa de Mundo. Tras un buen inicio, Alemania enfrentó a Italia en semifinales. Tal y como sucedió 26 años antes, en el Juego del Siglo, Alemania perdió en tiempos extras.

German fans are shown here watching their national team play during the 2006 World Cup.

Los aficionados alemanes miran un partido de selección durante la Copa del Mundo 2006.

19

The future of the *nationalelf* rests on players Lukas Podolski, Mario Gómez, and Bastian Schweinsteiger. With these players' strength and speed, Germany will remain one of the best national soccer teams in the world.

Jugadores como Lukas Podolski, Mario Gómez y Bastian Schweinsteiger son hoy el futuro del Nationalelf. Con su fuerza y habilidad, Alemania seguirá siendo uno de los mejores equipos de fútbol del mundo.

GERMANY  ALEMANIA

★ ★ ★

German Football Federation
Year Founded: 1900

―――――――――――――――――

Confederación Alemana de Fútbol
Año de fundación: 1900

 Home ←  Away

Local ← Visitante

Player Highlights / Jugadores destacados

Most Caps* / Más convocatorias

Lothar Matthäus (1980–2000)
150 caps / 150 convocatorias

* Appearances with the national soccer team

Top Scorer / Mejor anotador

Gerd Müller (1966-1974)
68 goals / 68 goles

Best Player / Mejor jugador

Franz Beckenbauer (1965-1977)
Winner / World Cup 1974 / European
Football Championship 1972 /
Ganador de la Copa del Mundo
1974 / Eurocopa 1972

Team Highlights / Palmarés del equipo

FIFA World Cup™/ Copa Mundial FIFA
  Appearances / Participaciones: 16
  Winner / Ganador: 1954, 1974, 1990
  Runner-Up / Segundo: 1966, 1982, 1986, 2002
  Third / Tercero: 1934, 1970, 2006

UEFA European Football Championship /
Eurocopa UEFA
  Winner / Ganador: 1972, 1980, 1996
  Runner-Up / Segundo: 1976, 1992, 2008

FIFA U-20 World Cup / Copa Mundial FIFA Sub-20
  Winner / Ganador: 1981

GLOSSARY / GLOSARIO

determination (dih-ter-mih-NAY-shun) Being firm in purpose.

dislocated (DIS-loh-kayt-ed) When a bone is not in its usual place.

exciting (ik-SY-ting) Very interesting.

World Cup (WUR-uld KUP) A group of games that takes place every four years with teams from around the world.

Copa del Mundo (la) Competencia de fútbol, cada 4 años, en la que juegan los mejores equipos del mundo.

determinación (la) Tener un propósito muy claro.

dislocado Cuando un hueso en el cuerpo se mueve de su lugar.

emocionante Muy interesante.

RESOURCES / RECURSOS

Books in English / Libros en inglés

Hornby, Hugh. *Soccer*. New York: DK Children, 2008.

Kalman, Bobbie. *Kick it Soccer*. New York: Crabtree Publishing, 2007.

Books in Spanish / Libros en español

Contró, Arturo. *Landon Donovan*. New York: PowerKids Press/Editorial Buenas Letras, 2008.

Dann, Sarah. *Fútbol en acción (Soccer in Action)*. New York: Crabtree Publishing, 2005.

Web Sites

Due to the changing nature of Internet links, PowerKids Press has developed an online list of Web sites related to the subject of this book. This site is updated regularly. Please use this link to access the list:
www.powerkidslinks.com/soct/germany/

INDEX

ÍNDICE